WATER POWER

A TRUE BOOK®

by

Christine Petersen

Children's Press®

A Division of Scholastic Inc.

New York Toronto London Auckland Sydney
Mexico City New Delhi Hong Kong
Danbury, Connecticut

The Grand Coulee Dam

Reading Consultant
Jeanne Clidas
*State University of
New York College*

Content Consultant
Tony Rogers
*Renewable Energy
Research Laboratory,
University of Massachusetts*

Library of Congress Cataloging-in-Publication Data

Petersen, Christine.
  Water power / by Christine Petersen.
     p. cm. — (A true book)
Includes bibliographical references and index.
Contents: Water on the move — Shaping the land — Electricity from
water — Ocean energy — Making a choice.
  ISBN 0-516-22808-0 (lib. bdg.)   0-516-21942-1 (pbk.)
  1. Water-power—Juvenile literature. [1. Water power.] I. Title. II. Series.
  TC147.P48 2003
  621.31′2134—dc22

                                        2003018340

Contents

Melting snow becomes part of a fast-moving creek.

Water on the Move

Every spring, an amazing change takes place high in the snow-covered mountains. It begins as a gentle *plink, plink, plink* that seems to come from the trees all around and from the deep snow underfoot. Soon the sound grows louder, changing to a trickle and then

5

to a splash. Warmed by the spring sun, the winter snow has begun to melt.

Rushing water from melting snow cuts paths through the snow and soil. It dribbles slowly downhill in response to gravity, the magnetlike force that pulls objects closer to Earth's center. Small trickles gather into streams, which join larger rivers farther down-stream. Swollen rivers boom down mountainsides and over

A natural stream of fresh water is called a river.

waterfalls, as loud and powerful as a freight train.

Eventually, mountain rivers
flow out onto the flatlands,

but the water's journey is not yet over. Rivers must still travel, sometimes hundreds of miles, to their final destination— the sea.

In the sea, water continues to move. **Ocean currents** are like giant rivers within the deep sea, carrying water to different parts of the ocean. **Tides**—the rise and fall of ocean water in response to the moon's gravity—cause the water to move higher and lower on the beach twice each

Water creeps up the shoreline.

day. Waves crash constantly against the shoreline.

However it moves—in rivers, waterfalls, currents, tides, or waves—water is a powerful force that shapes our planet. It also offers people an important source of energy.

The Water Cycle

Water molecules form when one atom, or tiny chemical particle, of oxygen joins with two atoms of hydrogen (H_2O). When cooled, gaseous water molecules high in the atmosphere gather together into clouds and fall as liquid rain or frozen snow, sleet, or hail. This precipitation fills rivers, lakes, and oceans, and some filters into the ground. Sun-heated water evaporates, becoming a gas that rises back into the atmosphere. Earth's water cycle goes on constantly, assuring that the planet has a steady supply of water in all three of its states—liquid, solid, and gas.

When the droplets become large enough, they fall to the ground as rain, hail, or snow.

Shaping the Land

Water is one of the most powerful forces on our planet. Caves, canyons, and cliffs are just a few of the natural wonders shaped by moving water.

The **energy** in rivers comes from **gravity,** which pulls water downstream toward the sea. In mountainous parts of the

Water erosion helped create the spectacular landscape of the Grand Canyon.

world, gravity makes rivers flow so fast that they "dig up" the surrounding land. This happens because rivers

River rapids wear away at granite rocks.

weaken the rock over which they flow, causing pieces to break off. The faster a river flows, the harder it can "dig." Over time, rushing water can cut a deep channel in the land. This is how canyons are made. Colorado's Royal Gorge is a stunning example. Carved into hard granite rock by the swift-moving Arkansas River,

The Royal Gorge and suspension bridge

the Royal Gorge is a narrow canyon about 10 miles (16 kilometers) long and 1,050 feet (320 meters) deep.

Tides are also caused by gravity. As the Earth rotates, part of the planet always faces the moon. Though the moon seems far away, its gravitational pull is strong enough to make seawater swell upward and away from shore. As the Earth rotates, the moon's gravitational hold on part of the planet is slowly released. Water then creeps back up the shoreline as high tide.

Waves are another form of moving energy. They usually begin when winds, far out over the open ocean, stir up water at the surface. Energy from the wind causes individual water particles to turn in circles, but the water doesn't actually move forward as it appears to. Instead, neighboring particles bump into each other like

Waves are created as a result of the interaction between wind and water.

falling dominoes in a line, causing the wave energy to travel forward. When a wave reaches shore, its energy has nowhere else to go. The heavy wall of water curls over and breaks.

Volcanic eruptions or earth-quakes on the ocean floor also create energy that is trans-ferred to the water. These sudden movements shake up waves that can be extremely large and fast moving.

Electricity from Water

Just as beavers build complex wooden dams across streams to create ponds, ancient engineers learned that dams are an excellent way to control the flow of water. Egyptians built dams across the Nile River 5,000 years ago to protect their cities from flooding.

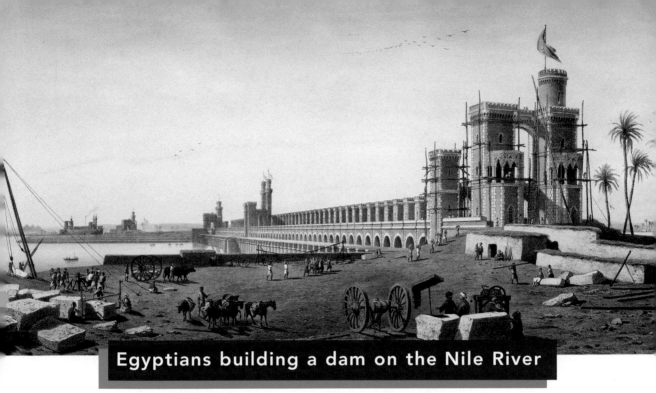

Egyptians building a dam on the Nile River

Today, there are more than 80,000 man-made dams in the United States. Dams block a river's path, usually causing water to collect in a **reservoir.** Dams and reservoirs make rivers easier to navigate, help hold

Ashokan Reservoir
in Shokan, New York

back floodwaters, and provide a
source of water for crops, cities,
and industries.

Although reservoirs look like
lakes, they contain river water
that is constantly trying to flow
downstream. Hydroelectric or
water-powered plants use the

energy of moving water in dammed rivers to produce electricity.

Water enters a hydroelectric plant through tunnels located near the base of the dam. Gates open and close to control how much water enters. Once inside the tunnel, water

The gates of the Bonneville Dam control the flow of the Columbia River.

is directed toward a **turbine** engine inside the dam. Like a fan or windmill, a turbine has blades that turn in circles. Rushing water causes the blades to spin. "Used" water is released into the river below.

The energy of the spinning turbine blades can now be converted into electricity. At the center of each turbine, a rotating metal shaft carries the energy upward to a **generator,** a circular magnet surrounded by coils of wire. The shaft turns the magnet,

causing electricity to flow into the wires. Electricity is then carried away from the plant through cables, providing power to cities and industries.

Modern hydroelectric plants can serve millions of customers. Nevada's massive Hoover Dam on the Colorado River is 726 feet (221 m) tall and contains seventeen generators. Lake Mead, the reservoir behind Hoover Dam, covers 247 square miles (640 square kilometers). With all that water power, Hoover Dam can provide electricity for 1.3 million people in Nevada, Arizona, and California. Around the world today, about 20 percent of all electricity is produced with hydro-electric power, or hydropower.

By supplying electricity to the nearby desert region, Hoover Dam made it possible for people to live there.

Regular electrical plants make use of water power, too. Oil, coal, or nuclear fuel is used to boil water, which produces steam. The steam expands, turning the turbines.

Machines that Changed History

A few thousand years ago, waterwheels were among the first tools used to make water power. They looked like wide wooden bicycle wheels. Water from a waterfall or stream pushed against paddles along the wheel's edge, causing it to spin. A metal rod connected the wheel to a millstone that ground wheat, oats, corn, or barley faster than a human ever could.

An historic water wheel at Sherbrooke Museum in Nova Scotia, Canada

Steam engine trains carried goods from one end of the country to another.

The invention of the steam engine in 1712 marked the beginning of a new era in industry. A single steam engine could do the work of many people, allowing factories to manufacture goods quickly, cheaply, and in large numbers.

Ocean Energy

Tidal energy was first harnessed almost 1,000 years ago. Ancient dams, built where streams joined the sea, used rushing water from the rising and lowering tides to run grain mills.

Today, a few experimental tidal power plants use a similar

A tidal barrage at Qanatar in Cairo, Egypt

idea. Tidal **barrages** are built across river mouths in parts of the world where water depth changes by 16 feet (5 m) or more between low and high tide. Just as in a regular hydroelectric dam, a barrage has gates that control the movement of water in and out of the plant. At high tide, water is held behind the dam. At low tide, water is released through the gates, passing through turbines on the way out.

Ocean Thermal Energy Converters (OTECs) are large experimental electrical plants that use the temperature of seawater to make power. The top of an OTEC reaches out of the water, and the bottom anchors to the seafloor. In

Some OTECs use ocean water and heat from the sun to produce electricity.

some OTECs, warm water from the ocean's surface causes ammonia or another fluid inside the converter to evaporate, producing steam to drive a turbine. Other OTECs actually boil seawater to make steam.

Scientists have also experimented with several methods of changing wave energy into electricity. One such method is the Salter's Duck, a kind of floating generator placed out in the open ocean. The name *duck* comes from the raft-shaped machine's ability to bob up and down like a duck atop the water. Waves constantly strike the generators, causing them to rotate and producing electricity that is transported to land inside waterproof cables.

Making a Choice

Today, most of our power comes from fossil fuels such as coal, oil, and gas. When burned, these are quick sources of energy. However, they are also found in limited amounts on our planet, and they cause a great deal of air and water pollution. Within the next 200 years, we

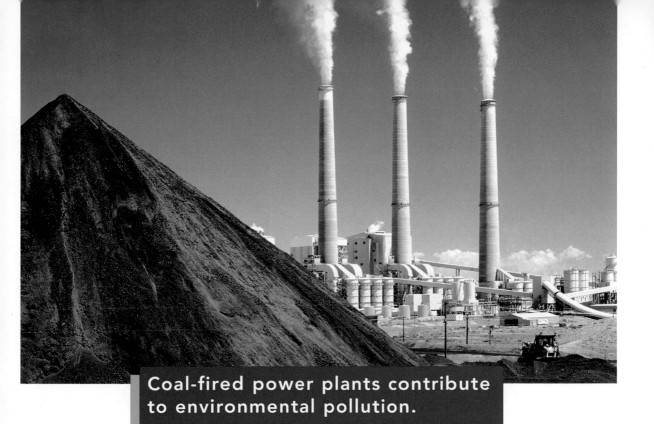

Coal-fired power plants contribute to environmental pollution.

are likely to run out of fossil fuels. Then we will need to rely on **renewable resources**—those that are constantly recycled in nature—to meet our energy needs.

Water is one of the most commonly used renewable resources. Many countries around the world, from Brazil to Norway to New Zealand, already use hydropower to make most of their electricity. Yet it is not a perfect form of energy. For example, hydro-electric dams can be harmful to the environment. When most new dams are built, a valley is flooded to form a reservoir. People who live in the valley

Workers build a reservoir
in Molokai, Hawaii.

Many people feel that the creation of dams and reservoirs disrupts the ecosystem, causing problems for birds and fish.

must move to new homes, and natural landscapes full of living creatures are destroyed. Even some of our most historic places have been buried underwater by reservoirs.

People and habitats down-
stream from dams are affected,
too. Water from hydroelectric
dam reservoirs is also used for
cities, crops, and industries.

Reservoirs provide irrigation water for
farmers in many parts of the country.

Everyone can make an effort to conserve water in their homes.

As a result, less water reaches the lower parts of the river. Sometimes so much water is "stolen" that the river no longer flows all the way to the sea. Conserving water by using less in our homes and factories is the only way to be sure that enough water is available for everyone.

Other forms of water power, such as tidal energy, may offer solutions that are less damaging to the environment. Unfortunately, tidal energy can only be gathered in the few places worldwide where tides are especially high. Tidal power plants also only function when tides are actively moving in and out, leaving them idle for as much as 16 hours per day.

Despite its problems, water
power is still an excellent energy
choice. Like wind and sun power,
electricity made from water
provides "clean" energy that
does not pollute our air or water
supplies. With time, scientists will

learn better ways to use these renewable resources. Renewables offer the possibility for lasting power—energy to light our cities and fuel our machines long after the last fossil fuels are burned.

The skyline of Louisville on the Ohio River

To Find Out More

Here are some additional resources to help you learn more about water power:

 **Books**

Gibson, Diane. **Hydroelectricity.** Smart Apple Media, 2002.

Graham, Ian. **Water Power.** Raintree Steck-Vaughn, 1999.

Hewitt, Sally. **Full of Energy.** Children's Press, 1998.

Parker, Steve. **Fuels for the Future.** Raintree Steck-Vaughn, 1998.

Tocci, Salvatore. **Experiments With Energy.** Children's Press, 2003.

Trueit, Trudi Strain. **The Water Cycle.** Franklin Watts, 2002.

Woodruff, John. **Energy.** Raintree Steck-Vaughn, 1998.

Organizations and Online Sites

Energy Story: Hydro Power
http://www.energyquest. ca.gov/story/chapter12. html

This California Energy Commission site contains an excellent history on the uses of water to create power.

How Hydropower Works
http://www.wvic.com/ hydro-works.htm

This Wisconsin Valley Improvement Company site explains how hydropower plants work.

Renewable Energy Resources from Earthdog
http://www.earthdog.com/ renew.html

This site has great background information on a variety of renewable energy sources, including water, wind, and solar power.

Energy Quest
http://www.energyquest. ca.gov/index.html

This California Energy Commission site is just for students, including the Energy Story, Science Story, and Science Projects. Meet scientists who study energy, and find out about the history of renewable energy.

Meet the Author

Christine Petersen is a middle school teacher who lives near Minneapolis, Minnesota. She has also worked as a biologist for the California Academy of Sciences, the U.S. Forest Service, the U.S. Geological Survey, and the Minnesota Department of Natural Resources, studying the natural history and behavior of North American bats. In her free time, Christine enjoys snowshoeing, canoeing, bird-watching, and writing about her favorite wild animals and wild places. She is a member of the Society of Children's Book Writers and Illustrators, and is coauthor of several True Books.